Then Morning Again

Then Morning Again

Poems by

Jane Ebihara

© 2025 Jane Ebihara. All rights reserved.
This material may not be reproduced in any form, published,
reprinted, recorded, performed, broadcast,
rewritten, or redistributed without
the explicit permission of Jane Ebihara.
All such actions are strictly prohibited by law.

Cover design by Shay Culligan
Cover photo by Tommes Frites on Pexels
Author photo by Julie Maloney

ISBN: 978-1-63980-749-9

Kelsay Books
502 South 1040 East, A-119
American Fork, Utah 84003
Kelsaybooks.com

for my sons,
Eric and Adam VanHyfte

Acknowledgments

Grateful acknowledgment is made to the following publications in which some of the poems in this collection first appeared:

Adanna Literary Journal: "Drought"
The Comstock Review: "Late Winter from My Window," "On Waking"
Dandelion Review: "What Felt Right" as "What Lingers"
Exit 13 Magazine: "Sated," "A Sense of Home"
Global Poemic: "Massage," as "Massage Post Pandemic"
Gyroscope Review: "Storm Warning"
Lips: "Turning Point"
The Orchards Poetry Journal: "Solstice"
Schuylkill Valley Journal: "Stray"
U.S.1 Worksheets: "Will It Never End?"

"Aubade," "Last Kiss," "Late Autumn" were published in *This Edge of Rain* (Kelsay Books, 2021).

"Last Kiss" was published in *A Constellation of Kisses* (Terrapin Books).

"Lesson from the Moon" was published in *A Reminder of Hunger and Wings* (Finishing Line Press, 2019).

"What Once Was" was published in *A Little Piece of Mourning* (Finishing Line Press, 2014).

Contents

Aubade — 13

I. Lessons in the Language of Loss

To Morning — 17
On Waking — 19
Drought — 20
Late Autumn — 21
Covid Surge — 22
Late Winter from My Window — 23
Massage — 25
Map of This Body — 26
What Felt Right — 28
Turning Point — 30
Yet Another — 32

II. Half a Light Is Whole Enough

What Once Was — 37
Marriage on Vacation — 38
Primed for Change — 39
Final Acts — 40
Storm Warning — 41
Spring Storm — 43
Lesson from the Moon — 44

III. This Will Become Memory

Today the Woods Are Theater — 49
Will It Never End? — 50
Songsters at the Poetry Workshop — 52
Dear Loneliness — 53

Last Kiss	54
Deja View	56
Once at Dusk	58
Sated	59
In This Late Life	60
Fault Lines	61
Squandered Thursdays	62
Taming the Wild Daisies	63
Something Like Gratitude	65

IV. The Pulsing Aria Within

Invocation	71
December Dawn	72
Stray	73
The Ruthless, the Devious, the Proud	75
Texas Storm	76
Taking Note	77
A Sense of Home	78
I'll Pass	80
And Once Again	82
Solstice	83

Aubade

the old woman in my mirror craves
little more now
than kinship with the living

she claims sisterhood with every fleeting thing
        slug and sparrow
        mite and minx
        seed and spore
        beetle and bear
the mighty and minuscule

the woman in the mirror savors
fire   laughter   the longed-for song
and language not her own

she leaves her meal
on the table
growing cold

hungers only
for morning
        then morning again

I

Lessons in the Language of Loss

To Morning

You draw me in like a lover
while the scent
of night still clings.

In the cool quiet
of your open arms
I curl, head upon your chest.
Hear your whispered
promise. Feel the rhythm,

the rhythm of the
untouched day.

Oh Morning,
it's best you leave me
each day. Best you

send me out alone
with your gifts wrapped
like newborns in my arms.

For were it *only* you,
I fear I would
soon long for

the noon-day rush,
the crush of hours—even
the wild accusations of the night.

I would tire of your incessant
listening, want you to speak
your mind. Challenge me.

I want no more from you than this—
your fleeting embrace,
our daily devotion.

On Waking

Was I pulled into this morning
by a barred owl's deep call—
a question escaping the woods?
Or was that a sound left
from the cinema of sleep?

Dreams settle, as memories do,
fallen sky on quiet water—
leave something real 'til waking
comes like breeze—returns
pond to pond, erases
the imagined.

Consider that book I couldn't find
on my shelf one morning—one
I had read only in sleep.

The heft of it in my palm so true,
the pale yellow pages filled with poems
I wanted to read again.

Morning lifts the lies the night
has conjured—a book, an owl,
an absent lover turning in the bed—
fades fact to fiction, disturbs reflection,
leaves behind only a piece of fallen sky.

Drought

Outside,
a jay screams. Daybreak
brushes the failed summer buds of the dahlias,
the ruined bee balm, the dust and stones. A doe
rests beneath my window—
quiet as an unspoken thought.

If there's a story in this thirsty day it's a quiet one
with a tea cup in it, or perhaps an avocado—
something offered in an outstretched palm.

Inside,
the room grows dark and the fan overhead
ruffles the pages of Dylan Thomas
and last Sunday's unfinished crossword.
My untouched journal opens and closes
in the rush of wind.

There's a sliver of light on the hallway floor.
Another jay scream. Today
I will plant asters next to the stump of the ash
that fell to borers last winter, deadhead the mums
and prune the catmint.

>there are a hundred
>words for *rain*—
>none of them fall on the garden

Late Autumn

Just yesterday the tree against the window
blazed in dusky light.
Autumn-rusted leaves graced the view.

Today the tree's stripped limbs arch
over a swell of faded pageantry—
burnt copper   tangerine   russet   bronze.

Summoning the alphabet I struggle
to recall the tree's name—I reach
the D's and the tree is a dogwood again.

I've been losing words. Not just names
of trees or people I once knew, but names
of things—
       kitchen tongs   nuthatch
       wheelbarrow   artichoke—

words I could do without, no doubt,
but winter nears—exposes
a horizon summer conceals.

Spring will return to soften the view, still
there is no word to stop the leaving.

This is what the seasons give,
lessons in the language of loss.

Covid Surge

I wake with relief from a dream
where someone was tying a tightrope
across a wide ravine—

the rope was thick and red like those
velvet ones used in museums
to keep visitors from touching
the past

many gathered for Thanksgiving
defying the advice of the learned

the rest kept caution from
the wind and held on to hope
for next year

we all walk the tightrope
some with tested step
some with a recklessness

that threatens to take us down

what I woke from was nightmare
what I wake to is real

soon enough
we'll know just how close
we came to falling.

Late Winter from My Window

My neighbors are moving today.
No longer safe their children say, she
having recently fallen, neither
able to drive.

A monstrous truck takes up the driveway—their life
hauled out and stacked like jigsaw into its gullet.

I want to be thinking of her, my friend, how much
she loves her home—the morning light
from her kitchen windows, the floral wallpaper
he hung for her, though he hated it so,
the deck where they sipped cocktails
while their voices shared the dying light.

I wanted to be thinking of her—how
this sudden turn has aged her overnight,
but I never thought *future* would knock
so soon, so near—invite itself in.

                        Instead of her,
I think of a stranger one day slipping a key
into *my* door, hanging a coat in my closet,
arranging tea cups in the cupboard . . .

It's raining now.

The movers pull away—
she stands in the driveway, watches
the truck disappear—an unopened umbrella
to steady her.

I'm suddenly desperate to look away—to turn
to my stack of unread novels, my uneaten soup
cooling in the bowl, my unpaid bills. Turn
to something . . . to everything unfinished.

Massage

this body no longer
barren limbs
reaching from shore
or even the motionless bank gloried
now in wild mustard weed
yellow as dawn

this body is river
running over sun-hot stone

carrying what breathes
the trout   the tadpole   the eel
cradling what floats and drifts

life   in motion
as before the drought

this body remembers
the brush of the fisherman's line
the swallows dipping
the rain tapping
the touching
the touch

Map of This Body

Early surveys show that borders
shift and plains erode,
slopes are flattened, trails obscured.
Charted paths still wind and turn—
traverse familiar fields once owned
by lovers, babes, young flesh and bone.

Artifacts—the scars, the stories carved in bone
break out forgotten borders—
reminders of chapters owned
by others who travel roads eroded
when unkind years turned
lush contours into roads obscured.

If you are lost, your route obscured
by time, recall the flesh, the bone
that drew you near before the turn
of seasons on these borders—
before the past eroded
what was owned.

Travel now as if these roads were owned
by memory alone, not past obscured
by loss, by tide, by time eroded.
The journey remains in marrow, in bone.
Wander, meander, span the borders,
explore the fields, the twist and turn.

Pause long enough before you turn
to hold warm earth no one's owned
but you—that no one's ever tamed with borders.
You'll know it for no scent's obscured.
What lives in buried bone
is fossilized—cannot erode.

Then pause again as past erodes
for soon it will be your turn
to leave your story carved in stone
then left in fields now owned
by those with tomorrow obscured
by boundary, barrier, border.

Borrowed bone and body both erode,
no border prevents the seasons turn.
The past is owned, the future still obscured.

What Felt Right

I stood in the kitchen doorway and listened.
My mother was instructing her grandsons—

they were making bread. *Push*, she said. *Push
with the heel of your hand, push and roll,
push and roll, You'll know when it feels just right.*

Later, she led them through her home—asking each
what he would like to remember her by once
she is gone. From her treasured,
she offered the drum table

with the leather trim she'd brought home
from Galloway's farm auction, Aunt Josie's

heavy lamp with its near-Tiffany shade
and the story of Uncle Harvey who *spoiled
Josie with such luxuries.*

Grandpa's pocket knives, her thimble
collection—even the silver one

that had graced her own mother's hand.
She was insistent. They were uncomfortable.

To please, they chose—
one a stiff horsehair love seat, the other

a wicker rocking chair—items neither
had interest in and neither claimed when she died.

She'd been gone for years when the younger
received a gift from his brother—

a single scented candle wafting vanilla
wrapped with a note-paper band

on which was carefully written,
Summer: Grandma's Kitchen

Turning Point

Thirty years since she's been on a bike,
my son must muse as I wobble away
alongside my grandson. Even without
a backward glance, I feel anxious eyes
on us as we slip from view.

This newly-minted teen whose chatter
has dwindled to mumble wants to show me
the path along the reservoir where he rides
after school each day.

Soon, with eyes glued to the trail ahead,
he begins to talk—

I'm not looking forward to school this year, he says,
as I pedal beside him, then tells of classes and bullies,
and how algebra will be easier than making friends.

Tell me when you want to go back, he says

> and oh, how I want to go back—to
> when I was useful for soothing fear,
> and smoothing sharp edges, when
> questions had answers and darkness held
> only imagined danger.
>
> *Sing me the song about today,* he would
> ask when I tucked him in at night—
> and I'd sing a litany of our day.

Gravel crackles under our tires, the lake appears, disappears and reappears through the trees. Revealing itself only in fragments.

This is where I usually turn around, I hear. So we do, pedaling back to the distant trailhead where my son stands—checking the time.

Yet Another

There have been 417 school shootings since Columbine.
  —The Washington Post, 09/24

It is the day after
when I take the path
along the Paulinskill,
the river high and rushing
from recent rains.

Nothing is broken here.

Armloads of wild phlox
rim the road with white
and shades of purple.

A lone angler stands
near the bank,
waist deep in the stream.

Three mallards take flight as one,
silent and swift, barely
a foot above the water.

Startled too, a trembling
of goldfinch—nine or ten
at least lift roadside
then settle in unison—

elfin flames high
in the limbs
of an arching willow

II

Half a Light Is Whole Enough

What Once Was

gather that around you
that you think will never change
name each one by one
the fur beneath your stroking palm
the palm
the bone china cup
the bone
the doe by the side of the road
the road
your child's sweet breath
the child
words like birthmarks on the heart
the heart
your lover's need
your own

Marriage on Vacation

each day they went
their separate ways

he
wandered empty beaches
captured photo-by-photo
sand canyons   hungry gulls
seaweed wound in twisted tapestry

she
pen in hand
untangled wounds
stitched words
to an empty page
mending mending

one morning as they dressed to go
she found his yesterday-sock
tucked inside her shoe

Primed for Change

Darkness seemed the spawn
of clouds and cold and
a planet tipped away from the sun.

When she brought home
the five-pound fan of paint samples,
primed for change, the long winter
was done.

She started in the bedroom
with a fine brush dipped in
Distant Thunder then trimmed
in *Tempered Steel* to keep
the veil of dark from falling.

The living room she painted
with broader strokes—from
Night Watch to *Thin Ice*.

It's Spring
yet the palette darkens,
Always Blue to *Misty Grey*
and she tiptoes through rooms
freshly coated
      with *Fisherman's Net*
      with *Solitaire*
      with *Stone*

Final Acts

He talked about
She talked with

He bargained for
She bargained with

He held forth
She held on

He longed to
She longed for

He leaned on
She leaned in

He shut down
She shut up

He slipped away
She slipped into

He let go
She let be

He gave up
She gave in

He went
She went on

Storm Warning

the birds are ravenous
charge the feeder like war planes
trained on enemy targets

foolish with plenty they
toss as much as they devour

this is not about hunger—
not about birds

there will always be days when
everything threatens to tear

days with questions
more ominous than forecasts
than clouds

days of *what if*
days of *what then*

following days
of *enough*
too much

this would always be true

it keeps returning—
the day he said no
to tomorrow—
pushed everyone away

and she flew
wingless
into the fist of a storm

Spring Storm

Gray clouds precede the wind
that stops and starts again—
teasing the morning.

The dogwood tosses
her confetti gown,
strips down to bare limbs, cups
her leaves, inviting the darkening
sky to satisfy her thirst.

Her blossoms heap
in piles about her trunk,
gather in the birdbath,
settle on the stone wall
beyond. Still,

bold as the very wind
that blows, she bows
to the coming storm.

Lesson from the Moon

how whole a half can be
half a dream still a dream
half a song lives on
half a meal can satisfy
half a moon shows how
    half a light
is whole enough

III

This Will Become Memory

Today the Woods Are Theater

Wind rocks the wren house,
birds shelter in the sway
of limbs. What lives hides,
imagines breath invisible in air.

Here, carried on a curtain of wind,
the cold rattles everything to life

and you return—still silenced—
as if there were nothing left to say.

Will It Never End?

When will I stop getting mail for a man
eight years dead? He has no need
of hearing aids, investment advice,
or a new roof.

Staunch Democrat though he was, he's unlikely
to contribute to any campaign
and his vote not likely to be cast.

The ash of him scattered
here, and there—

a handful to a California tide pool,
fistfuls in the Jersey Atlantic,
and more in Chester's sunflower field. The rest buried—

by the bird bath outside the kitchen window,
fed to a sapling pear in the Catskills, and spread
under an oak on the path to Black River—scattered
with the ashes of the hounds we walked there.

The cleome thrive around the birdbath,
the pear tree blossoms, the oceans slap
against their shores—offering him up over and over.

The sunflower field's plowed under now,
it's pumpkins this year—
enhanced perhaps with a whisper of flesh, of bone

of a man
who no longer worries, hungers, regrets or dreams,
a man who doesn't care if his car warranty has expired.

Songsters at the Poetry Workshop

Through the window I watch
two doves build a nest
under a covered porch.

They are a team,
one in the nest while
the other comes and goes.

Just feet away I sit
in a stiff-backed chair
and try to listen to talk
of cadence and meter,
rhythm and tone,

but it's birdsong I hear,
call and response.

One cocks her head
the way birds do—
perhaps she listens

for our song—the one
we've yet to lift
from the page.

Dear Loneliness

Spiteful sister of Solitude
now perched upon my chest,

who asked you here to brood—
dark, uninvited guest?

Why bring your discord now (so rude)
to my just-feathered nest?

I was content before you blued
the night, the light, the rest.

Your sweet sibling you have shooed
in this your selfish quest.

Have you no idea how you are viewed?
I always liked her best.

Last Kiss

First, in your seventies and alone, you read that those who
count such things say an average person kisses for a total

of two weeks in a lifetime. And you realize your two weeks
was up some time ago. Suddenly there is kissing everywhere

you look. And you learn that cows kiss and squirrels. Puffins,
snails and meerkats! And you are overcome with sorrow and

an overwhelming desire to kiss—to be kissed. And you learn
that's called basorexia and you have it. You watch the lips

of strangers in the supermarket—wonder if one would want
to kiss you. You know now that a minute of kissing burns

twenty-six calories and that a man lives up to five years
longer if he kisses his lover before he goes to work. You want

to tell someone that. And what's worse, unlike the first kiss,
the last slipped by unnoticed. It might have been

a spring day when daffodils answered the sun's invitation or
an autumn day when everything else was burning. Or simply

a day you took out the garbage, did a load of wash. Then, someone
comes and takes your hand and you remember words

to a song you thought you'd never hear again and you remember
all those sunsets you forgot to watch and the smell of woods in rain

and you remember the river, the river—how it presses its mouth
again and again to the swollen sea.

Deja View

that near-belief that if we return to the place where we once saw it,
the fox, the pheasant, the bear, the newborn fawn may reappear—

as if memory were magic. As if we have seeded the countryside
with recollections—left them to germinate and bloom again when

next we passed by. We expect a porcupine, a pulsing field of
fireflies, a coyote in the rear-view mirror. Expect they have

lingered like ghosts on roads that wind through farmland,
woodland, and hills we call mountains here. Roads named

Bear Creek, Long Bridge, Quaker Church, Thunder Mountain.
Roads where we saw kingfisher in the sod field, flocks

of goldfinch, sandhill cranes, a rookery of heron. Roads
where we lingered to hear a chorus of peepers, pull ramps

in the woods, taste a soybean, rescue a turtle. Roads
where we captured photos of wildflowers with names like tiny

poems—Jewel Weed, Wild Asparagus, Bitter Winter Cress, and
Poison Hemlock masquerading as Queen Anne's Lace. Roads

where we talked with Nam and Suki pulling leeks from their field,
to Mike who tells us there is an albino fawn in his yard,

and to Farmer Joe astride his tractor who won't live
through the next harvest. We meet Lynn who says

there are bobolinks in the unplowed fields and we wave to the
migrants hand-planting peppers who gesture us closer to watch.

Roads where we eat our lunch any place by a river,
Paulinskill, Pequest, Delaware.

a flash of bobcat
an explosion of snow geese
fox kits at play

Once at Dusk

we park on a country road
huddled in the vanishing day
binoculars trained on a fallow field

watching for short-eared owls

frosty December air fills the car
the sun slides behind the hills—
promises abandon

you tell me the owl's flight will be silent—moth-like—
wings flapping high in a slow floppy fashion
and that their color will resemble the dried
grasses of the field

evening light falls on an empty sky
and you hold my hand until the darkness comes

the mice and vole of the field
are spared tonight

from a stealthy hunter's slow flap and hover
the drop   the kill

this will become memory

still we will return
for clarity in darkness
       a meteor shower
       a streak of comet
       fireworks splattering the hills

Sated

While sharing an apple in the car, I asked, *What was the most memorable piece of fruit you ever ate?* And you told me about the cooked Koudougou chicken you once bought through the window of a train in Burkina Faso—how it was too spicy to eat, how an old man sitting across from you saw your dilemma and pulled three tangerines from his bag—an offer to trade for the chicken.

Memory.

Shared like grain from an open palm—the train, the open window, the unbearable spice of the chicken, the yearning to taste it, the trade. Those sweet, sweet tangerines.

In This Late Life

We cannot name each flower in the field
know every star that hangs above,

why must we speak of love?

Offer me no vows—
language fails in this late light.

our summers dwindle.

No promise can adorn the meadow,
no syllable enhance the sky.

Let's walk the wild grassland
that blooms under nameless stars

and talk about tomorrow
as if it could be ours.

Fault Lines

The earth shakes/just enough/to remind us.
—Steve Sanfeld

First it was the sound—a faint distant rumble
that approached from my right, grew louder
as it neared. Were I a city dweller
I would have thought *subway* in a tunnel below.

But there are no subways in this peaceful rural valley.
Here where we savor the absence of change.

First, it was the sound.
Then an awareness—shuddering
walls where picture frames rocked
then resettled askew.

Ancient Greeks thought Poseidon was angry,
Japanese myth blamed Namazu, a giant catfish
who it was said lived beneath the surface of the earth.

Here first thoughts were common nouns—
furnace? jet? truck? wind? Not *earthquake*.
Not here.

Some things are not supposed to fail—sunset, moonrise,
foundations—the ground on which we walk
and sow and sleep, not meant to shake
us from complacency one ordinary day while we stir
cream into a trembling cup—

not meant to warn us of the fault
we've lived with all along.

Squandered Thursdays

I have spent over 4,000 Thursdays in my life—

spent them like pennies glinting on the pavement
that no one bothers to retrieve. Spent them like stones

tossed in the river, like dandelion fluff shaken
in the wind. Spent them as if they had no value, as if
I would never have need of another.

It's another Thursday. The day is young, the room
darkened by gathering clouds, a threat of rain.

Had I a journal of my Thursdays—there must have been
one when at this hour I was making love or making oatmeal,

a Thursday when I was late for school, in bed with measles,
kneading bread. One when I nursed a baby, raked a pile of leaves.

All those failed memories, all those Thursdays buried now—like
bones of something that once was whole.

Taming the Wild Daisies

After days of rain, the garden is now lush
and chaotic at once. Weeds run amuck—bully
any buds that struggle to share the sun. A single
columbine stands tall, its pastel bonnets bowed
as if shamed by its own audacity to rise
in the crush of weeds and *daisies!* So many
daisies.

An army of daisies has conquered the garden—answer
to a bag of seeds that once boasted, "a showcase
of varied blooms year after year." And I that lazy
gardener who sparked the revolution.

Please know I do respect the daisy—its staunch simplicity
and plucky display of persistence, but I've become ruthless—
yank hands full of stalks and, what I pray are weeds,
to create breathing room for other blooms, ones fallen
victim to the invasion.

With judgment clouded by ignorance, sentencing is senseless—
if it slides too easily from the bed, it must be a weed,
or something too weak to survive. If it has to be dug out or clipped
it's *surely* weed. To those I say aloud, *I know you'll be back,*
for I speak as I pillage.

Neighbors must think me mad—hunched and muttering
in the tangle of possibility. *And, what are you? Weed
or wildflower? Last year's coreopsis, poppies, cosmos, lupine?*

I have made of this plot of earth a cliche, a hostile country,
and of myself a tyrant. I ravage and rule—seeking order
in the chaos I've created. Cursing the wild I meant to love.

Something Like Gratitude

The gray sky had just begun
to clear as we abandoned
our search—no snow geese today.

We'd hoped to witness their riotous
flurry of white in an empty field.

Headed home a patch of woods caught
our eyes—barren limbs of January trees
bristled with life and a harsh metallic concert—
grackles—oft maligned outcasts
of the avian world.

We stopped to watch and listen

when, as if in response to a director's
baton, they spread their glossy wings
and, en masse, rained onto the cornfield
below. Hundreds
             falling,
                        falling to feast—
a squall of iridescent splendor.

Hand-in-hand, astounded by our
good fortune, we watched in silence.

We're good at this, it seems—finding
what we didn't know we were looking for—
the "we" of us as unexpected as this
theater in the field

Soon,

the throng lifted their black curtain
in near-murmuration—swooped
and curved as one before lighting again
in the shadowed arms of the waiting trees,

their deafening cacophony
charging the air with something
resembling celebration—something
like gratitude.

IV

The Pulsing Aria Within

Invocation

I rise early now and walk alone
to birdsong and soft shower,
to brush of wing in meadow overgrown

and in the quiet morning roam
the lush and waking bower.
I rise early now and walk alone.

I share a forest's quiet undertone—
a crunch of leaf, a wildflower,
the brush of wing, the meadow overgrown.

I linger here by brook and stone,
embrace the dayspring power,
rise early now to walk alone.

I hear swish and crack of life unknown,
snake, sparrow and fawn that cower
mid brush of wing in meadow overgrown.

Too soon it's time to turn for home
to introduce the rush, the hour.
I rise early just to be alone
with brush of wing and meadow overgrown.

December Dawn

I had not yet embraced the inevitable winter
that gray morning the robins came.

In those numbers, it's said, they are a *blush*—
suggesting shyness, timidity, quiet—a poor name
for this avian rave that crowded in the juniper boughs
until the the limbs sagged and the tree pulsed
and throbbed as if the birds were its beating heart.

The tree's berry-like cones
became banquet so plentiful the frosty
ground below seemed to blossom
into discarded purple promises
to spring.

Severing the silence with frenzied jubilance
robins spilled by the dozens
onto the lawn with song and squabble,
jockeyed for room at the birdbath,
jabbed at the cold earth, retreated,
returned, trading perches, trading song,

infusing the break of day
with jubilance.

Stray

Mornings I watch you lumber by.
Your graceful strides, your effortless leaps
slackened now by a belly
that sways to your four-beat gait.

You are heavy with young. Lost,
abandoned or born in the wild—to a world
that barely admits you are here.

And even I only conjure your life,
invent you in memory.

You, crossing this quiet street,
slipping like something
dreamed into the woods

where vole, chipmunks and birds
scatter, wary of your feral ways.

These woods where soon you'll
find a place to lay down
your parcel of easy prey.

Little warrior, little saint,
I've carried no burden like yours,
faced no such loneliness.

    Forgive my arrogance—
how I dare surmise your hardship,
assign imagined doom
to the young you are soon to suckle.

How useless I am to you—full of pity
and meaningless mercy.

The Ruthless, the Devious, the Proud

Look how I've assigned gratitude to the cardinal
who splashes in the freshly filled bath—how

she surely thanks me for my thoughtfulness.

Yesterday, I watched a jay wing-sprawled on the fence rail—
Cocky, like a young man leaning on the bar, I thought.

The wren attributes no blessing for the house I hung,
the nuthatch no resentment for the empty feeder.

It is we who spend our days searching for reason,
we who woo with words when song

might be enough. We who cannot watch
the soaring raptor without thinking him,

ruthless, devious, proud.

It is we who envy, who hope and praise. We
who know guilt and love and regret.

We ignore them, dismiss them, devour them—
they know no envy, no judgment, no shame.

Who are we to level them so?
It is they who were given wings.

Texas Storm

We do not inherit the earth from our ancestors,
we borrow it from our children.
—Native American Proverb

Ice numbs this southern
city into submission, coats
every tree then clings
until even the mighty oaks succumb—
their massive trunks torn from the soil,
burdened limbs snap
leaving whole neighborhoods darkened,
but for the luminous temple
of wounds shimmering
under a gibbous moon.

This wreckage—minor inconvenience
when weighed against heatwave,
hurricane, drought and wild blizzards
that punch back in the war
we have waged on our planet.

Evidence of our squandered legacy.

Taking Note

I'm curled in quiet, book in hand
when sudden birdsong invades
the room insistent
that I take note

and I'm returned to that time
at the library when I heard

someone singing—
not humming softly with reverent nod
to the silent space, but singing
with full-throated, voluptuous sound.

Bold as a bassoon in a chapel
unapologetically out of place.

And I, who covet the quiet the library offers,
I, who follow the rules to a fault,
was flooded with unexpected gratitude.

This is the memory that comes
to me now as the cardinal tosses
his song into the still evening.

Reader, reader, he seems to call
as I put down my book, press
palm to chest—reminded

of the pulsing aria within.

A Sense of Home

for Bart

The new neighbor sweeps
his white-tipped cane
from one edge of the sidewalk
to the other. His face lifted
to the sun.

He makes his measured way
around the block—listening
his walk home.

Does he hear the soft scuttle
of squirrel, the woodpecker
tapping, the wing-whistle
of a dove taking flight?

Perhaps it's scent
that evokes his smile—
freshly mown grass, needles
of pine, woods still damp
from recent rains.

Surely, he reads each
curve in the walkway
each incline, each crack
in the cement. Maybe
he counts each step.

He's out of my sight now.

I close my eyes, *see* him
tap to his door, reach
for the knob, then turn
for one last taste
of this September sky.

I'll Pass

        each morning
        a committee of clouds
        designs a new day

The word is out—I'm *old.*
Glossy brochures fill my mailbox
with promises of idyllic habitats—
The Elms, The Pines, The Willows.
offering grand living—
Villas, Estates, and Manors,
or for those with a more humble aesthetic—
Gardens, Meadows, Hills—suggesting
a peaceful transition to a final resting site.

Seems it's a common belief
that those in my *condition* long to join
smiling seniors who grace the panels
of snappy fold-outs. Classes too—

flower arranging and origami, sing-alongs,
film nights, jig saw puzzles, lectures, and field trips.
Imagine.

I toss a recent mailer in the bin, step barefoot
in nightgown onto my deck. A doe and her fawn
prune my hosta just feet away, a hummingbird whirs past,
sun throws morning light onto the bed of daisies
I seeded years ago. A woodpecker drums in the woods,
chipmunks chase over the rocky wall where wild berries
climb the split rail fence ripe and ready for picking.

    evening
    blankets your ashes
    beneath the marigolds

And Once Again

morning

a swath of dark wings
punctuates the hush of sky

rips open the still
water below
leaves behind a story
for sky and lake to share

it's an old tale
titled *Today*

untouched
yet pregnant
with possibility

Solstice

to the fog that softens sharp edges
shields the distance clings to the darkness

to the Long Night Moon that hasn't yet
finished its shift

to the deer who forage these woods
and turn their backs to me,

to the wind that whips the pines
interrupts the shadows   then stops
as if to catch another breath

to the birds I know are here
but shelter in silence
high in these trees
to the hot cup in my hand
the blaze of the fire   the warm
socks on my feet and a new year near

I give thanks

to the berries on my neighbor's holly
that squirrel sprawled on the split rail fence
the frost on the lawn
and the contrail of a jet overhead

where someone is leaving
where someone is coming home

About the Author

Jane Ebihara was born and raised in Illinois before moving to New Jersey in 1977 where she taught middle school literature for 26 years before retirement. She has been a recipient of a Geraldine Dodge Fellowship to The Fine Arts Work Center in Provincetown, MA and a volunteer author for Senior Life Stories Project sponsored by New Jersey NORWESCAP. Currently, she is an active participant in two poetry workshops and, along with poet Elaine Koplow, hosts two quarterly poetry venues in rural Warren and Sussex County, NJ. Additionally, she serves as an Associate Editor of *The Stillwater Review*.

Jane's previous books are *A Little Piece of Mourning* (Finishing Line Press, 2014), *A Reminder of Hunger and Wings* (Finishing Line Press, 2019), and *This Edge of Rain* (Kelsay Books, 2021). Her poems have been published in multiple poetry journals and anthologies and are often inspired by the beautiful countryside of rural northwest New Jersey, where she lives.

Website: janeebihara.com
Email: jeeb@optonline.net

www.ingramcontent.com/pod-product-compliance
Lightning Source LLC
Chambersburg PA
CBHW030911170426

43193CB00009BA/810